MW01600222

# SUMMARY OF
# WHERE THE CRAWDADS SING |

# NOVEL BY
# DELIA OWENS

**abayomi raheem**

INTRODUCTION:

The tale's main account opens in the marshland near the fictional town of Barkley Cove, North Carolina. Seven-year-old Catherine "Kya" Clark lives in a shack in the swamp with her mother, father, and siblings. However, one day, Kya's mother leaves the shack forever in order to escape the physical abuse inflicted by Kya's father. Kya's siblings soon leave on their own as well, leaving only Kya and Pa. Pa spends progressively more time away from the shack over the years, and when Kya is about ten years old, Pa leaves forever. Kya has become thoroughly self-sufficient by this time, living on the land and occasionally trading in town for necessary supplies.

When Kya is 14 years old, a kind local boy named Tate Walker begins to visit Kya, and he instructs her how to read. He is about four years older than Kya. He also gives Kya his old textbooks from school. When Kya is 15 years old, she and Tate fall in love, however Tate insists that they do not have sex until Kya is older. Tate soon leaves for school, and although he promises to love and remember Kya, Kya feels abandoned. At the point when Kya is 19 years old, she suddenly moves toward becoming attracted to a young nearby man named Chase Andrews. Chase starts visiting her often. Chase says that he loves her and is eager to have sex with her. Kya refuses at first, yet after about a year, she consents to sex.

Tate eventually returns to Barkley Cove in order to perform scientific research on the marshland. He visits Kya and asks for forgiveness, yet she refuses to take him back. Tate sees that Kya has performed much of her own research on the marshland, and he urges Kya to submit it to publishers. Tate also warns Kya that Chase is a dishonest womanizer. One day, Kya sees in the paper that Chase has become engaged to someone else. She is heartbroken. Later, she submits her research to publishers, and when she is 22 years old, a book of her examination is published under her name. Kya's brother Jodie sees the book in a store and returns to the swamp to reconnect with Kya. Jodie encourages Kya to give Tate another chance.

Chase eventually visits Kya and says that he wants to continue his relationship with her, despite the fact that he is married to someone else. When Kya refuses him, Chase tries to rape her. She hits him and get away. Kya realizes that because Chase is such a popular member of the town, and because she is an outcast for living in the swamp, she has no recourse. One day, in October of 1969, Chase's body is found near the swamp. He shows up to have fallen—or possibly have been pushed—out of a flame watchtower. The sheriff researches and arrests Kya. However, the evidence is inconclusive and circumstantial, and Kya is acquitted. She and Tate declare their love for each other, and they live together in the swamp. Kya continues her career as a naturalist, and Tate continues his career as a researcher. Kya dies at age 64, after which Tate finds proof that seems to prove that Kya slaughtered Chase. He disposes of the evidence so that no one will ever find it.

## PLOT SUMMARY

In The tale's main account opens in the marshland near the fictional town of Barkley Bay, North Carolina. Seven-year-old Catherine "Kya" Clark lives in a shack in the marsh with her mother, father, and kin. Be that as it may, one day, Kya's mother leaves the shack always so as to escape the physical abuse inflicted by Kya's father. Kya's kin soon leave on their possess too, leaving only Kya and Dad. Pa spends progressively more time far from the shack over the years, and when Kya is about ten years old, Pa leaves forever. Kya has become altogether self-sufficient by this time, living on the land and occasionally trading in town for fundamental supplies.

When Kya is 14 years old, a kind local kid named Tate Walker begins to visit Kya, and he shows her how to read. He is about four years more seasoned than Kya. He also gives Kya his old textbooks from school. When Kya is 15 years old, she and Tate fall in love, however Tate insists that they do not engage in sexual relations until Kya is more seasoned. Tate soon leaves for school, and although he guarantees to love and remember Kya, Kya feels relinquished. At the point when Kya is 19 years old, she all of a sudden progresses toward becoming attracted to a young nearby man named Chase Andrews. Chase starts visiting her often. Chase says that he cherishes her and is enthusiastic to have sex with her. Kya refuses at first, yet after about a year, she consents to sex.

Tate eventually returns to Barkley Cove in request to perform scientific research on the marshland. He visits Kya and asks for forgiveness, however she refuses to take him back. Tate sees that Kya has performed much of her own research on the marshland, and he urges Kya to submit it to publishers. Tate also warns Kya that Pursue is a dishonest womanizer. One day, Kya sees in the paper that Pursuit has move toward becoming engaged to another person. She is grief stricken. Later, she submits her research to publishers, and when she is 22 years old, a book of her exploration is distributed under her name. Kya's brother Jodie sees the book in a store and returns to the swamp to reconnect with Kya. Jodie encourages Kya to give Tate another chance.

Pursue eventually visits Kya and says that he wants to continue his relationship with her, despite the fact that he is wedded to someone else. When Kya refuses him, Pursue attempts to rape her. She hits him and get away. Kya realizes that because Chase is such a popular part of the town, and because she is a outcast for living in the swamp, she has no recourse. One day, in October of 1969, Chase's body is discovered near the swamp. He appears to have fallen—or possibly have been pushed—out of a flame watchtower. The sheriff examines and captures Kya. However, the proof is uncertain and circumstantial, and Kya is acquitted. She and Tate declare their love for one another, and they live together in the bog. Kya continues her career as a naturalist, and Tate continues his vocation as an analyst. Kya kicks the bucket at age 64, after which Tate finds proof that seems to demonstrate that Kya slaughtered Chase. He disposes of the evidence so that nobody will ever find it.

# SUMMARY

The prologue opens near the town of Barkley Cove, North Carolina. It is October 30, 1969, and the recently dead body of a man named Chase Andrews is on the ground near the marsh. Chapter 1 opens in August of 1952. Catherine "Kya" Clark, the protagonist, is six years old and lives in a shack in the bog with her parents and her four older siblings. One day, Kya's mother leaves the shack, never to return. No one in the family speaks of Mama's departure, however Kya spends each day on the steps, waiting for Mama to return. Her older brother, Jodie, helps distract her by playing with her. In Chapter 2, over the next couple of weeks, Kya's siblings all leave the house to live on their own. Kya knows that they are leaving because they do not wish to live with Pa. Kya wonders why none of them took her with them. Pa, a veteran of World War Two, begins to leave the house for quite a long time at a time. On those days, Kya takes care of herself by cooking food from the garden and strolling to Barkley Cove to buy food. At some point, in town, she sees a boy named Pursue Andrews. Soon, Kya's seventh birthday arrives.

Chapter 3 takes place in 1969. Some local young men accidentally find the body of Chase Andrews, and they go to tell the nearby sheriff, Ed Jackson. Sheriff Jackson, inspecting the scene, notes that Pursuit obviously fell to his death from the neighborhood fire tower. Also, strangely, there appear to be no footprints other than the ones left by the boys who discovered the body. In Chapter 4, it is harvest time of 1952, and Kya is mostly living by herself. One day, a truant officer arrives at the shack and takes Kya to the school. Kya has never been to school before. At school, the other kids scorn her in light of the fact that she lives in the bog. Kya chooses never to return to school, and she stows away at whatever point truant officers or other officials arrive at the house in the following days.


Chapter 5 takes place in 1969. Sheriff Jackson discusses the crime with his agent, Joe Purdue. Chase had been a star quarterback in high school, and as a grown-up, he was a womanizer. Jackson and Purdue wonder if Pursue's womanizing had anything to do with Pursue's death. They don't decide out the truth that Chase's death may have been accidental. Chapter 6 takes place in 1952. Kya takes out Pa's speedboat for an exploratory ride through the marsh waters. She encounters a boy who recognizes her as Jodie's sister. The boy looks to be around 10 or 11 years old. Kya has become lost, and the boy, Tate Walker, helps direct her home. Tate then returns home to his father, a bereaved, poetry-loving fisherman whom everybody calls Scupper. Tate mentions that he has been enjoying examining biology in school. Scupper peruses some poetry to Tate, and Tate finds himself pondering his experience with Kya earlier that day.

## ANALYSIS

The original foundational element of Kya's account seems to be a state of surrender and independence, as the flight of her family members fosters a state of solitude and necessary independence from a early age in Kya's life. At this point in the novel, the account remains somewhat cryptic about the reasons for the family members' departures. However, there is simply enough detail to permit readers to make inferences. First, Mama withdraws, and then each of Kya's siblings depart. At one

13

point, the narration states that Kya "knew Dad was the reason they all left" (13). Dad is not yet shown to be specifically abusive, yet the peruser may infer that Pa has been physically and/or mentally abusive towards his family. That previous line of narration is then pursued with this line "… what she wondered was why no one took her with them" (13). Kya is inevitably left completely alone in the shack in the swamp, and thus she must rapidly adapt to a real existence independent from anyone else. Out of need, Kya teaches herself how to cook, manage the garden, and go to town for supplies. Throughout the novel, this state of confidence and independence dominates Kya's life and standpoint.

Kya's sense of solitude and independence is further engendered by her feeling of distance from surrounding society, as the episode

14

involving her day at school exhibits the bias she faces due to the circumstances of her birth. Kya goes to school for one day on the grounds that a truant officer arrives to bring her to school. However, Kya finds the lessons and activities strange, and she experiences criticize and humiliation from the other students. The students explicitly insult Kya because she lives in the marsh. The kids chant things like, "Where ya been, marsh hen? Where's yo' hat, swamp rat?" (30). For these reasons, Kya chooses never to return to class, and she shapes a much more profound bond and feeling of self-identification with the marsh. Thus, between Kya's abandonment by her family and her alienation from the surrounding society, Kya becomes specifically bonded to the marsh and the swamp. The main contrasting component is Kya's interaction with Tate Walker. Tate does not seem to hold prejudice against Kya, and he is even kind and helpful towards her. Along these lines, the novel foreshadows the bond that develops between them all through the account.

Meanwhile, the novel starts fabricating a parallel narrative that appears to have only a couple connections to the main narrative, however these associations and the general quality of mystery create an air of suspense and curiosity that help to propel the reader and keep them alert. While the main narrative proceeds in a linear design starting in 1952, the parallel story starts in 1969 after the body of Pursue Andrews is found. Before the end of the novel's first few chapters, there are only two connections between these accounts: one area and one character. Pursue Andrews makes a short appearance as a boy in Part 2, and his body is found 17 years later near the marsh where Kya lives. These associations may lead the reader to suspect that Kya may have been included in Chase's demise, however all details relating to a possible motive are clouded from both the peruser and the sheriff. Joe Purdue makes reference to that Chase was a womanizer: "Tom-cattin', ruttin' 'round like a penned bull let out" (38). Thus the reader may try to start solving the mystery, yet the lack of facts and proof leaves the reader in a state of suspense.


Chapter 7 takes place in 1952. Kya, in the shack, thinks about Tate and about her expanding isolation. Pa eventually returns, and Kya makes a dinner for him. The next morning, Dad and Kya in go in Pa's watercraft to go fishing. They go fishing nearly every day, and Kya hopes to encounter Tate again. One day, Pa says that his family used to be wealthy and live in Asheville. Part 8 takes place in

1969. Sheriff Jackson informs Pursue's folks and Chase's spouse Pearl of Pursue's death. One day, Jackson overhears two locals tattling and saying that Pursuit could have been murdered by "that woman lives out in the marsh" (62), however Jackson pays the gossip no mind. Chapter 9 takes spot in 1953. Pa and Kya go to the Gas and Bait store, owned by a black man whom everyone calls Jumpin'. Pa and Kya eat in a restaurant. A lady advises her daughter not to go near Kya. Later, Pa disappears again for a couple days. Kya thinks about the times that Pa, inebriated, beat Kya, her kin, and Ma. Pa eventually returns and finds a blue letter sent via mail. Kya thinks it is from Ma, and to Kya's unnerve, Dad burns it before leaving again.

Part 10 takes spot in 1969. Jackson and Purdue go to examine the wrongdoing scene again however find nothing. They wonder if tidewater may have cleared the sand of impressions and other conceivable evidence. Chapter 11 takes spot in 1956. Kya is ten years old, and Dad has been spending more and more time away from the shack. The supply of money in the shack starts to run out, so Kya uncovers mussels from the sand and moves them to Jumpin'. In Part 12, Kya continues to live on her own. She once in a while sees Tate, yet she always watches him from a far distance rather than speak to him. One day, she sees a group of children joyfully playing. Among them is Chase Andrews. Kya eventually begins fishing as well so that she can trade the fish in town for supplies. Jumpin' helps her arrange exchanges.

Section 13 takes spot in 1960. Kya is 14 years old and living alone in the shack. She begins collecting interesting specimens from the bog, such as bird feathers. One day, a group of young men sees her, and they all ridicule her and call her feral. She runs away. Section 14 happens in 1969. A lab report confirms that Pursuit died from falling. The lab examination additionally finds strange red filaments on his jacket. Chapter 15 takes place in 1960. Kya goes looking for plumes in the swamp once more, and she is surprised to see a quill set on a stump for he, along with a milk carton containing some useful supplies. One day, she stands by the stump and sees Tate approach. She thanks him for the gift, and he offers to teach her to read. In Chapter 16, Tate teaches Kya to read, and the portrayal briefly exposits upon the economic decay faced by Kya's parents amid the Incomparable Depression.

ANALYSIS

The novel further develops and emphasizes Kya's sense of distance by showing how antipathy form individuals in town drive Kya to further retreat into the seeming wellbeing of her habituated condition in the swamp. As Kya continues to become more independent, she continues to develop a stronger connection with the swamp. Additionally, Kya's sense of home in the swamp proceeds to frame her as an object of fear and ridicule in the eyes of the townspeople. For example, when Kya and Dad eat at a restaurant, a woman in the restaurant says to her little girl, "don't go near that girl, ya hear me. She's filthy" (66). The woman's antipathy and aversion towards Kya seems to be based not strictly in the conviction that Kya is literally dirty, yet more saliently in the belief that Kya is bizarre and corrupted because she has such a different background. Kya's origins and life are so strange and

unfamiliar to the townspeople that
the townspeople respond with
distrust, antipathy, and aversion.
This idea is further accentuated when
a group of boys encounters Kya in the
woods and call her names like "Marsh
Young lady" (91) and "Miss Missin'
Connection" (91). This sense of fear
and hatred may likewise add to the
townspeople's prompt suspicion of Kya
when Chase Andrews is discovered
dead.


Kya's alienation progresses toward
becoming even more trenchant as she
becomes increasingly alienated from
her family and from her family
history, as Kya's identity moves
toward becoming increasingly reliant
not on family connections or stories,
yet more on her present conditions of
survival and self-reliance. Kya
learns a little about her family
history when, one day, Dad suddenly
says to her, "My folks weren't

generally po', ya know" (57). He then provides some broad insights concerning the previous wealth of his family. Work in Chapter 16 provides further context for this riches and decline, demonstrating Pa and Mama's personal financial decrease during the Great Depression. However, in light of the fact that Kya's family members all in the long run leave her, Kya has no persistent association with her family or her family history. Pa's destruction of the mysterious blue letter appears to be a strike against a conceivable transformation of a family connection. Dad then deserts Kya permanently, and her familial alienation progresses toward becoming complete. This familial alienation appears to be a final step in Kya's decline into complete separation, as she becomes an individual almost completely devoid of societal connection.

However, Kya's isolation is contrasted by two staying societal connections—Tate and Jumpin'— and the benefits and fulfillment that Kya receives from these connections demonstrate the indelible necessity of interpersonal connection. Firstly, Kya's connection with Jumpin' is beneficial not just in a practical capacity, yet in addition in an emotional capacity. Jumpin' is indicated to be kind, thoughtful, and helpful towards Kya, just out of the goodness of his heart. He is thoughtful towards her, and his practical support towards her seems to be symptomatic of enthusiastic help, thoughtfulness, and sympathy as well. Tate speaks to another positive connection to the outside world. He is also kind towards her and holds no prejudices. He instructs her how to read, and he is never restless, unkind, or mocking towards her. As the portrayal states, "He didn't want to shame her" (105), as he did not want to be unkind or make her uncomfortable. Through these character connections, the story exhibits the passionate and reasonable necessities of having of constructive relational connections in one's life.

Chapter 17 takes place in 1960. Kya goes to Jumpin's store, and Jumpin' says that individuals from Social Administrations have been asking around town about Kya. Jumpin' lied to the authorities and said that Kya's father was still living with her. Kya tells Tate this news, and he says he knows of an abandoned cabin in the marsh where Kya can hide for some time. Over the late spring, Tate continues to teach Kya how to read. Tate inevitably starts teaching Kya verse, and Kya appreciates poetry very much. Tate starts his senior year at high school and brings his old textbooks for Kya to read. Kya understands them with enchant and curiosity. One day, Kya starts enduring from stomach spasms, and Tate tells her that she is having her period. It is Kya's first period, and she goes to Jumpin's spouse Mabel for help. One day, when Tate is visiting Kya at the cabin, Kya and Tate all of a sudden kiss. They decide to be boyfriend and girlfriend.

Chapter 18 takes place in 1960. Tate continues to visit Kya to give her lessons in various subjects, such as math. On Kya's fifteenth birthday celebration, Tate brings her a birthday cake and presents. One day, in the winter, Tate's father says to Tate that he realizes that Tate has been visiting Kya in the swamp. He warns Tate against impregnating Kya. Tate indignantly informs his father that he and Kya have never had sex. One day, in the spring, Kya attempts to initiate sex with Tate. However, he refuses on the grounds that Kya is just 15 years old. Tate maintains his love for Kya. In May, Tate informs Kya that he will be going to college in House of prayer Hill, North Carolina to study biology. He says that he will visit her frequently. He says that he will never overlook her and will never stop loving her.

Chapter 19 takes place in 1969. Patti Love, Pursue's mom contacts the sheriff's office and says that she has something that may be valuable to the investigation into Chase's demise. Part 20 takes place in July of 1961. Tate has already left to work in Chapel Hill before college. Despite the fact that Kya has been abandoned before, she seems to be especially heartbroken by Tate's departure. In the shack, she screams and cries and appears to fear that Tate will not return to her. Section 21 takes place in 1961. Still in a state of sadness, Kya begins to wonder if something about her drives people away. Kya turns out to be much more reclusive and goes into town as meager as possible. She begins to feel very forlorn. She spends her time collecting specimens of nature from the swamp. Chapter 22, happens in 1965. Kya is 19 years old and still living alone in the bog. She sees Chase Andrews one day and feels a faint physical attraction towards him. In the interim, at school, Tate has move toward becoming devoured with study and research, and he feels that he ought to no longer visit Kya because she is from such a different world.


## ANALYSIS

Kya's romantic and sexual awakenings include a layer of complication and external dependence to her presence, as she becomes dependent on the outside world not only for periodic supplies and companionship, yet also for potential sustenance of her newly discovered sexual and romantic drives. Kya's newfound self-identification as a woman is the biggest principal change in her self-perception since her family relinquished her. She not only undergoes the biological transformation of having her first period, however she also undergoes the transformation of building up a drive towards sentiment and sexual want, both specifically aimed towards Tate. These drives become nurtured by Tate's reciprocal love and sexual want. Tate even says to Kya, "I cherish you" (135). Be that as it may, the fulfillment of these attractions seems to eventually be stymied by considerations of age and social division. Kya wishes to have sex with Tate, however Tate refuses due to the fact that Kya is only 15 years of age. Also, the steadiness of their loving relationship is disrupted due to Tate's movement to

Chapel Hill for school. Thus, while Kya's sexual and romantic arousals seem to add a greater drive towards connection with others, they likewise appear to create a greater limit for disappointment.

The profundity and importance of Tate's departure mark a deepening of Kya's reclusion from society, as Tate's departure specifically echoes the departure of Kya's family, and the ensuing torment appears to drive Kya towards further reclusion. Although Kya seemed to endure feelings of pity and fear following her family's abandonment of her, her pain following Tate's takeoff appears to be considerably more intense. She returns to the shack, where she screams and cries. This overflowing of emotion seems to be symptomatic of a profound feeling of pain and betrayal; Kya had grown to love Tate profoundly, and along these lines his departure marks a intense tragedy and disappointment for Kya. The takeoff drives Kya into further reclusion. As the narration states, "For a month… Kya did not leave her place, did not go into the marsh or to Jumpin's for gas or supplies" (145). Kya then went into town as little as possible and continued to live in a state of near total isolation for years. These actualities mark an extending of Kya's disconnection, as the torment of Tate's saw double-crossing seems to have further distanced Kya structure any expectation of having a fulfilling interpersonal connection.

When Chapter 22 portends a possible interpersonal connection between Kya and Pursue, the narrative seems to emphasize the certainty that Kya's fascination towards Chase is of a desperate and physical quality, in this way far removed from the romance and fulfillment that seemed to be guaranteed by Kya's relationship with Tate. At the point when Kya watches him from afar, the portrayal states, "her body watched Pursue Andrews, not her heart" (150). Therefore, Kya's conceivable attraction towards Pursue appears to be merely physical rather than passionate or romantic. However, and fundamental emotional component may be inferred by the reader in that Kya's years of isolation may have intensified her desire for some type of interpersonal association. Thus, although Kya has developed into a potentially embittered, lonely young lady, she may be developing an attraction towards Pursue due to an instinctual drive towards sentimental and/or sexual friendship.


Chapter 23 takes place in 1965. One day, Kya encounters Chase in the marsh. They spend the rest of the day together and even kiss. Pursue attempts to initiate sex. He is aggressive. Kya hits him and runs away. In Part 24, Chase visits Kya at her shack the next day and apologizes for his actions. Kya pardons him, and they go to the nearby fire tower to look at the bog from above. Kya gives Pursue a shell jewelry that he made. They then go to Kya's shack, and Chase is impressed with the numerous specimens that Kya has found and named. Pursue says that he is fascinated by Kya and likes her very much. Kya feels a stir of trust in adoration. Chapter 25 takes place in 1969. Patti Love, Chase's mother, visits the sheriff's office. She says that Pursue always wore a shell necklace that was supposedly a present form Kya, however the necklace was not on his body when his body was found. Patti says that the sheriff should investigate Kya.


Part 26 takes spot in 1965. Pursue starts visiting Kya regularly. They invest energy together in the marsh, never in town. They kiss however do not have sex. Tate has graduated from college and is now in graduate school. He has arranged to center his research on marshland nature. He has also acknowledged that he adores Kya and needs to marry her. However, when he visits her, he sees her with Chase and leaves. Using library books, Kya has become very knowledgeable about biology, ecology, and zoology. Chase says that he is falling in love with Kya and needs to have sex with her, however Kya does not wish to have sex. She asks when Chase will introduce her to his companions and guardians, and he says that he will soon.

Chapter 27 takes place in 1966. Kya and Chase have been together for about a year. Chase suggests that they build a place of their own on the edges of town. He suggests that she come with him on a trip to Asheville. In Asheville, they stay in a motel. Chase says that they should have sex, and Kya agrees, however she finds the sex unsatisfying. Afterwards, Kya asks when Chase will he will begin consolidating her into the rest of his life. He says that it is to some degree complicated, yet he will soon. A few months later, Tate visits Kya's shack to ask for absolution. He additionally says that Chase is going out with other ladies around the local area. Kya, angry at Tate, advises him to leave. Tate advises Kya to send her gathered samples to a publisher for cash. Chapter 28 takes place in 1969. Sheriff Jackson talks to an angler who says that he saw Kya on her boat heading towards the fire tower on the night of Pursue's death. Chapter 29 takes spot in 1967. Pursue continues to visit Kya. They have sex, however the sex is never satisfying for Kya. One day, Kya sees in the paper that Pursue has become engaged to marry a woman named Pearl.


ANALYSIS

Kya's growing love for Chase marks a resurgence of expectation for an association with the outside world, demonstrating the certainty that Kya's basic desire to connect with society is innate and can't be destroyed by disappointment or abandonment. Kya has suffered many crushing abandonments in her life, from her parents to her siblings to her Tate. However, as she progresses toward becoming increasingly attracted to Tate, he builds up a renewed trust not just for love, however also for a possibility to consolidate herself into life beyond the bog. The portrayal states that with Chase, Kya starts to feel "The first trust in her heart since Tate left" (169). Kya evidently can't free herself of the intrinsic human want for connection, and Chase's consideration appears to have reawakened that desire in her. Additionally, Chase's consideration appears to promise the idea that Chase will help to consolidate Kya into town life. As the narration states, "Kya began to picture him taking her on a picnic with his companions. All of them snickering, running into the waves" (184). Kya is excited by the possibility of finally being acknowledged by outside society with Chase's help. Pursue fuels Kya's trusts by saying that he does plan on introducing her to his friends and family at some point.

Be that as it may, as the account continues, Chase's genuine nature of inconsideration, manipulation, and selfishness becomes increasingly clear, thereby foreshadowing yet another example of betrayal and torment for Kya. Pursue repeatedly guarantees that he will introduce Kya to his companions and guardians, yet he makes no actual strides towards doing so. Besides, the peruser has already been alerted in Section 5 to the fact that Pursue is a womanizer. Further evidence of Chase's dishonest ways is presented in Section 27 when Tate says to Kya, "You don't live in town. You don't know that Chase goes out with other ladies. Just the other night I viewed him drive away after a gathering with a blonde in his pickup. He's bad enough for you" (197). The reader may infer that Tate is possibly lying so that Kya will break up with Chase. Be that as it may, Tate has not appeared to be deceptive or untrustworthy in the past, apart from his deserting of Kya. In any case, when Kya sees the article about Chase's commitment, Tate's accusation against Chase demonstrate to be genuine. Thus these elements of foreshadowing are critical for building to the revelation and to Kya's resulting feelings of pain and betrayal.

The proceeded with advancement of Tate's storyline bears a blend of hope and tragedy, for although Tate personally recommits to his love for Kya, his abandonment of Kya may have permanently harmed the healthy, loving relationship that they had shaped previously. While in college, Tate became persuaded that his and Kya's lives were too different for them to be together. In any case, he in the long run realized that he could not stop cherishing Kya and that he wanted to be with her forever. Shockingly, the pain of his abandonment still deeply affects Kya. At the point when he at last visits her again to ask for pardoning. Kya yells at him in a fury. Tate then concedes, "You're directly about me, Kya. Everything you said is valid… I'll never bother you again. I just need to apologize and clarify" (197-198). Thus, it seems that the emotional damage of Tate's treachery may be indelible. However, the possibility of inevitable reconciliation between them remains a black out however tireless source of narrative hope.


Chapter 30 takes spot in 1967. Kya is extremely upset following the revelation of Chase's marriage. She realizes that she has been used and controlled. She calms herself somewhat by reciting poetry by Amanda Hamilton, a writer. Chapter 31 takes place in 1968. Kya is now 22 years old. A book written by her—The Ocean Shells of the Eastern Seaboard—is scheduled to be distributed soon, and she looks forward to composing more books. She has become highly knowledgeable in her field due to her self-lessons. Kya gives a copy to Jumpin' and also sends a copy to Tate. Kya learns that her family owns the marsh, and she plans to pay the back taxes on it with the cash from her books. Tate visits Kya one day to tell her that he read her book and that it is extraordinary. Chapter 32 takes place in 1969. Sheriff Jackson learns that, on the night of Chase's death, Kya was in Greenville to meet with her distributer. This appears like a strange coincidence to Jackson. Also, the bus schedules show that she could have taken a bus back in the night and then returned to Greenville before daytime, so Jackson decides to request a warrant to seek Kya's home.

Chapter 33 takes place in 1968. Jodie abruptly arrives at the shack. He is a war veteran and is now attending college. He saw Kya's book in a store and chose that he needed to visit her. He asks for forgiveness for relinquishing her, and Kya forgives him. Kya recalls physical abuse that Pa inflicted on his wife and kids. Jodie says that he does not know

where any of the other family members
are except for Mama, who died two
years prior of leukemia. Kya is
deeply saddened by the news. Kya and
Jodie talk about their lives and
about adolescence. They agree that
Mama likely left to escape Pa's
misuse. Kya talks about Tate, and
Jodie encourages Kya to forgive Tate
and have a relationship with him.


Chapter 34 takes place in 1969.
Jackson and Purdue arrive at Kya's
home in the marsh. She is not there.
They look through the shack, and they
find a red cap. Filaments from the
hat are indistinguishable to the
fibers from the crime scene. Chapter
35 takes place in July of 1969. Kya
thinks about Tate and considers
Jodie's recommendation that if Kya
loves Tate, Kya should give Tate
another chance. Section 36 takes
place in 1969. Jackson and Purdue
consider Kya's possible rationale,

yet they are unconvinced that being jilted by Chase is enough of a motive for a capture. However, after a man named Rodney talks with them, they choose that they have enough of a motive for an arrest. (The narrative does not yet uncover what data Rodney conveyed.) In Part 37, it is December, 1969. Jackson and Purdue trap Kya while she is in her watercraft and arrest her. Part 38 takes spot in 1970. Kya is on preliminary for murder, and if she is sentenced, she may receive the death penalty.

## ANALYSIS

The materialization of Kya's successful profession as a naturalist stands as further sign of her personal abilities and worth, and thus the novel further demonstrates how the townspeople's antipathy and prejudice towards Kya was unwarranted and unjustifiable. Even before the production of Kya's book, the novel shows Kya as a kind and fit individual, despite the fears of the townspeople. Kya is able to live on her very own in the swamp, and in spite of the scorn and persecution of the townspeople, she has proven herself fit of love and loyalty. Moreover, her self-lessons have showed her own significant capacity for learning and hard work. Kya is so dedicated in her love of nature and her study/exploration of it that she is capable to start a profession as a naturalist in her early twenties, despite having no formal tutoring. Tate even says, in the wake of perusing her book, "Kya, your book is a wonder" (221). Kya's career success is not a necessary component of proving that she is a significant person and deserves dignity. However, her success does help to work against the townspeople's false, out of line, biased notions of her as a feral, subhuman entity.

44

The reappearance of Jodie helps Kya process her past and the import of her family connections, and Kya's forgiveness of Jodie shows how interpersonal redemption can be guaranteed even after surrender years of separation. Jodie seeks out Kya after he sees her book in a store, and he asks for forgiveness for abandoning Kya. Kya excuses him and seems charmed to be brought together with her sibling. She is then disheartened to learn of her mother's death. Kya says, "I've had no family, no news of family for most of my life. Presently inside a few minutes I've found a brother and lost my mother" (238). Although this moment is quite tragic, it also reaffirms the esteem of family connections in Kya's eyes, for she is glad to be brought together with Jodie, and she feels the gigantic loss of her mom's death. Additionally, with Jodie present, Kya at long last has someone

45

with whom to discuss the salient occasions of her childhood, such as Pa's abuse of the family and Ma's possible takeoff. Although it is painful to dredge up these memories, it seems to be a remedial process for Kya, allowing her to come to more direct terms with the difficult and candidly scarring parts of her childhood.

As difficulties mount for Kya, Tate still functions as a potential source for hope and love, and the narrative seems to position Kya and Tate's relationship as a central hope for true and enduring happiness in Kya's life. After Kya tells Jodie about Kya and Tate's history, Jodie encourages Kya to give Tate another chance. Jodie says, "Let's face it, a lot of times love doesn't work out. Yet even when it fails, it connects you to others and, at last, that's all you have, the associations" (242). Jodie says that because Tate recognized his imprudence, and in light of the fact that love still appears to exist between Kya and Tate, at that point Kya should give her relationship with Tate another shot. Thus, even as Kya must face her criminal preliminary, Tate appears to speak to the likelihood of hope.

Chapter 39 takes place in August of 1969. Chase visits Kya in the bog. He says that he needs to resume his relationship with her. When Kya refuses, Chase hits Kya and tries to assault her. Kya hits him in the gonads and flees. She notices two men in a watercraft who saw the struggle. Chapter 40 takes place in 1970. The prosecutor calls to the stand Rodney Horn, one of the two men who witnessed the struggle. Rodney says what he saw. When the guard attorney cross-examines, he has Rodney reiterate the truth that Chase was attempting to rape Kya and that Kya was defending herself. Chapter 41 takes place in August, 1969. Kya fears countering from Chase, and she knows that the townspeople and police will not help her, as Pursue is a well known member of the community, and she is an outcast. Chapter 42 takes spot in 1970. Kya is in a prison cell between trial sessions. She helps calm herself by reciting poetry to herself.

Chapter 43 takes place in September, 1969. Kya gets an invitation from her publisher to meet with him in Greenville. Tate visits Kya and notices the bruise on Kya's face inflicted by Chase. Kya does not tell Tate about the attempted rape. In the following days, Kya lives in fear of Chase and tries to figure out what she ought to do. Chapter 44 takes place in 1970. Before the preliminary, the prosecution offers a supplication deal for limited correctional facility time, however Kya chooses to go to trial. Later, Tate visits Kya in the jail to comfort her. Chapter 45 takes place in 1970. The trial proceeds. The prosecution calls the area coroner as an observer. The coroner affirms proof, for example, the red fibers, that underpins the conclusion that Kya may have slaughtered Chase by pushing him through the trapdoor in the flame tower. However, the defense lawyer then cross-examines, and the coroner affirms that the evidence is incidental, that there is not indisputable evidence, and that the red filaments may have been exchanged to Pursue at any time during his association with Kya.

Chapter 46 takes place in September of 1969. Jumpin' sees the bruise on Kya's face. Kya makes Jumpin' promise not to tell anyone that Pursuit attacked her, as she knows that everybody will side with Chase and further persecute her. Jumpin' agrees not to tell anyone. Section 47 takes place in 1970. The trial continues. The prosecution calls Sheriff Jackson as an observer. On the witness stand, Jackson talks about the suspicious lack of impressions and fingerprints at the crime scene. During interrogation, Jackson admits that it is possible that Chase fell by accident and that the fire tower was a security danger. In Chapter 48, Kya leaves for Greenville in late October, 1969, and she returns two days later. When she returns, Jumpin' tells her that Pursuit was found dead. In Chapter 49, during the preliminary, the defense attorney questions transport drivers who say that they are do not remember seeing Kya on any bused on the night of Chase's demise.

ANALYSIS

As the novel progresses, the narrative maintains a careful balance of uncertainty regarding Kya's guilt or honesty, thereby maintaining both intrigue and momentum in the story. As the mystery and procedural components of the book start to take focus, the account takes on more accentuated elements of the puzzle and thriller genre. Moreover, the narrative deftly gives alternating evidence for and against Kya's guilt so as to keep the reader engrossed and uncertain. For example, this dynamic can be viewed in the procedural elements of the court scenes, as the prosecution interviews witnesses and then permits the defense to interview them in agreement with standard lawful procedure. With each observer, the prosecution builds evidence apparently in backing of Kya's guilt, and then the defense shows how none of the proof is conclusive. For model, the coroner states that "the evidence would support that end"

(295) that Chase was killed. Be that as it may, during questioning, the defense lawyer demonstrates that just because proof potentially underpins a conclusion does not make the evidence conclusive. Another example is when Jackson is on the witness stand. He emanates a belief that Kya is certainly blameworthy, yet during cross-examination, he must admit that it is possible that Chase fell accidentally.

As the account develops Kya's conceivable motive for killing Chase, the narrative does not necessarily assert that Chase deserved to die, yet the story does examine the possible relationship between's Chase's awful actions and Kya's sense of dread. When Chase endeavors to rape Kya, the full depth of defilement in his character is uncovered. Chase not only lies to and manipulates women, yet his sense of qualification apparently can drive him to violent activities such as endeavoring rape. This attack leads Kya to a state of significant fear. The narration states, "Pursue would not let this go. Being isolated was one thing; living in fear, very another" (284). This narration dynamic can additionally be read as conveying specifically feminist themes, for Kya has no plan of action against her attacker in part due to male benefit and partiality against women. This account dynamic capacities to simulate the sense of defenselessness that women often face in instances of sexual assault, as sexism and prejudice often weight plan of action against the victim.

Kya's position of powerlessness not only demonstrates elements of sexism, however it is likewise formed by the dynamics of prejudice that the novel has explored since exceptionally early in the story. As the narrative has shown, the townspeople see Kya as an outcast. Conversely, the townspeople view Chase as one of their own, however also as one of their most beloved members. As Kya says to Jumpin', "you know how it is. They'll take his side. They'll say I'm simply working up trouble… It would end in enormous inconvenience [for me]" (302). Jumpin' and Tate, both realizing that Kya is correct in this appraisal, concur not to tell anybody about Pursue's assault on Kya. In this way, the novel exhibits how benefit can shield a person from appropriate equity for wrongdoings. Thus, if Kya did kill Chase, the murder would likely have been motivated by this realization that there was no other recourse by which to secure her own safety.


Chapter 50 takes spot in 1970. The prosecution calls Patti Love to the stand. She gives declaration about the shell neckband that Chase always wore, which was a gift from Kya and which was not discovered on his body. The prosecution presents an artwork that Kya made and gave to Pursue. The painting delineates Kya and Chase in the flame tower together. In Chapter 51, the indictment calls a fisherman to the stand. The angler testifies that he saw Kya on her boat heading towards the fire tower on the night of Chase's death. Nonetheless, during cross-examination, the fisherman says that he cannot state with full certainty that it was definitely Kya that he saw. In Part 52, the barrier calls to the stand a lady who saw Kya board a transport to Greenville on the afternoon of October 28, 1969. The defense then calls the proprietor of the Greenville motel where Kya stayed. The owner says that he never saw Kya leave her room on the night of Chase's demise. Be that as it may, on cross-examination, he admits that she could have slipped out without him noticing.

In Chapter 53, the arraignment and defense each give their closing contentions. In his closing argument, the defense attorney emphasizes the lack of indisputable evidence. He also stresses the reality that Kya has been unfairly persecuted as an outsider for her whole life, and he frames the trail itself as a side effect of that persecution. In Part 54, the jury deliberates and reaches a verdict: not guilty. Numerous spectators in the courtroom are disillusioned by the decision. Kya is deeply relieved. In Section 55, Jodie brings Kya back to her home in the marsh and implores her not to give up on humanity, despite all of the injury she has encountered. Kya considers his advice however reaches no conclusions. Later, she sees the sheriff and Tate, and it looks like the sheriff is taking Tate into custody. In Chapter 56, Kya and the reader learn that the sheriff was simply illuminating Tate that Tate's dad had died. Tate mourns at his father's grave and then goes to Kya. They announce their everlasting love for one another.

In Part 57, Tate proposes marriage to Kya. Kya rejects the thought of formal marriage and says that they are already married. Tate moves in with Kya in her home in the bog. Kya never goes into town once more, however she keeps thinking of her books. As time passes, community sentiment changes in favor of Kya, and people concur that she never ought to have been arrested. One day, Jumpin' bites the dust, and Kya grieves him, as he was like a dad to her. Over the years Kya continues her work, and Tate sets up his own lab in his and Kya's home. They attempt to have children, yet they unfortunately

are never fruitful in doing so. Kya
dies at the age of 64. Tate then goes
through her belongings and discovers
that the nearby poet, Amanda
Hamilton, was actually Kya, composing
under a pseudonym. He likewise finds
the shell neckband that Kya gave to
Chase. Tate realizes that Kya really
did execute Chase. Tate throws the
necklace into the water so that no
one will ever find it.

ANALYSIS

The defense attorney's closing
arguments help to thematically
emphasize the nature of persecution
and antipathy, both towards Kya and
in general, for the lawyer empowers
both the peruser and the jury to see
how the preliminary is symptomatic of
that persecution. The safeguard
lawyer not only points out the need
of decisive evidence to convict Kya,
yet he also frames the trial as a
moral coming up short in itself. As
the peruser knows, Kya has been the
victim of general persecution for her
entire life, as other individuals see

her as an outcast despite her kindness, affectability, and knowledge. The safeguard attorney shuts his contentions by stating, "It is time, at last, for us to be reasonable to the Swamp Girl" (341). Despite the fact that, as the reader later learns, Kya really did execute Chase, the resistance attorney is essentially correct in his evaluation. Kya was arrested without conclusive evidence, to a great extent due to the unjust biases against her. This dynamic demonstrates the degree to which prejudice can overturn standards of fairness and morality. Moreover, the mental and enthusiastic toll of such bias weighs heavily on Kya, for when Jodie encourages her not to give up on humanity, she isn't prepared to so right away.

The adventure of Kya and Tate's life following the preliminary seems to reaffirm Kya's general decency and personal worth, and keeping in mind that Kya is not free of moral defect, the novel presents the probability that persecution and injustice were the genuine roots of evil in the story. In the years following the preliminary, Kya and Tate are able to have a fulfilling life together as cherishing partners. They live together in the swamp and lead productive lives, contributing to logical knowledge. In addition, although Kya does not become a section of the surrounding community, the townspeople look more generous on her: "As time passed, most everyone agreed the sheriff never should've arrested her. After all, there was no hard evidence against her, no genuine proof of a crime. It had been genuinely merciless to treat a shy, characteristic animal that way" (360). A reader may argue that because Kya really did kill Pursue, she isn't morally justified in any way. Nonetheless, one may additionally argue that Kya had no decision, as it was her only recourse to defend herself, and that those non-ideal moral conditions were made by the atmosphere of persecution that surrounded her.

At the end of the novel, Tate and

the peruser learn that Kya really did kill Chase, and this revelation forces the reader to confront the moral tensions created between the inherent unethical behavior of murder and the factors that drove Kya to the act. Slaughtering Pursue appears to have been the only immoral act that Kya ever committed in her life, and she felt that she had no decision yet to murder Chase in request to protect herself, both from Pursue and from further persecution by the community. On one hand, a reader may argue that the fact of Kya's blame supersedes all other moral considerations and that she should have been arrested and sentenced for the crime. On the other hand, the arrest and trial itself were actually born on motivations of prejudice instead of conclusive evidence, and additionally, Kya had no other means by which to protect herself. The narrative seems to leave this ethical inquiry open-finished for the peruser's thought, however the elements of persecution that worked against Kya still remain specifically relevant in portraying the

impropriety     of     out     of     line
persecution.

CPSIA information can be obtained
at www.ICGtesting.com
Printed in the USA
LVHW091121210619
621926LV00049B/127/P

9 781070 555799